SCOTT COUNTY LIBRARY SYSTEM

Both Sides of the Story

ANIMAL RIGHTS

ANIMAL RIGHTS

Patience Coster

rosen publishing's
**rosen
central**

NEW YORK

This edition first published in 2013 by:

The Rosen Publishing Group, Inc.
29 East 21st Street, New York, NY 10010

Copyright © 2013 Arcturus Publishing Limited

First Edition

All rights reserved. No part of this book may be reproduced in any form without permission in writing from the publisher, except by a reviewer.

Editors: Nicola Barber and Joe Harris
Picture researcher: Nicola Barber
Designer: Ian Winton

Picture credits:
Corbis: 11 (Karl Ammann), 27 (Najlah Feanny), 41 (Charlie Mahoney). Science Photo Library: 8 (CCI Archives). Shutterstock: cover left (Ivonne Wierink), cover right (Dario Diament), title page and 29 (Tomasz Bidermann), 7 (Paul Prescott), 12 (Losevsky Pavel), 14 (anyamay), 17 (Picsfive), 18 (RGtimeline), 21 (Lucia Pitter), 23 (KROMKRATHOG), 24 (Iculig), 30 (Vladimir Melnik), 33 (Natalia Mikhaylova), 35 (Randy Rimland), 37 (Diane Garcia), 38 (Wolfgang Kruck), 42 (A7880S).

Library of Congress Cataloging-in-Publication Data

Coster, Patience.
Animal rights/Patience Coster.—1st ed.
   p. cm.—(Both sides of the story)
Includes bibliographical references and index.
ISBN 978-1-4488-7184-1 (library binding)
1. Animal rights—Juvenile literature. 2. Animal welfare—Juvenile literature. I. Title.
HV4708.C67 2012
179'.3—dc23

2012023102

Manufactured in China

SL002125US

CPSIA Compliance Information: Batch #W13YA: For further information, contact Rosen Publishing, New York, New York, at 1-800-237-9932.

Contents

Different From Us?

Planet Earth is a populous place, inhabited by millions of species of animals—from the enormous blue whale to microscopic organisms. Over thousands of years, the human animal has gained dominance over other species. Today, many humans use animals or their products for food and clothing, as beasts of burden, in entertainment and medical research and for companionship. But should the fact that humans have bigger brains and greater skills give them the right to use animals as they wish? Or should animals, like people, have rights under the law?

Until relatively recently, the rights of animals were fairly low on the agenda. Life was cheap and the struggle to survive was bloody and brutal. One stark example of this struggle is that of the passenger pigeon. As recently as 200 years ago the passenger pigeon was the most common bird in North America. During the late 19th and early 20th centuries it was hunted on a massive scale because it provided cheap, easily accessible meat for poorer people. The hunting was catastrophic for the birds, resulting in extinction when the last passenger pigeon died in 1914.

Welfare versus rights

During the 1600s a few people began to campaign against intentional cruelty toward animals. Eventually animal welfare laws were passed in a number of countries. The aim of these laws was to prevent unnecessary cruelty to animals. While few people today would argue against the idea of

The "five freedoms"

- freedom from hunger and thirst

- freedom from discomfort

- freedom from pain, injury or disease

- freedom to express normal behavior

- freedom from fear and distress

animal welfare, the subject of animal rights attracts passionate defenders and opponents. The principle of animal rights is that the basic needs of animals—the right to life, to freedom from suffering and from captivity—should be given the same consideration as those of humans. These rights for animals under human control have been set out in the so-called "five freedoms" (see panel, page 6).

Since the 1970s, a growing number of people have begun to insist that many "higher" animals (primates in particular) should be regarded as nonhuman "persons" entitled to rights, like people. Meanwhile there are still many who believe that animals exist simply for humans to use as they see fit. For most people, the answer lies somewhere between the two extremes.

Ponies carry heavy loads through a Himalayan mountain pass. Some humans treat beasts of burden, such as horses, donkeys and mules, as members of the family, but many animals are cruelly mistreated and neglected.

Without feeling?

In the 17th century, René Descartes, a French mathematician, philosopher and scientist, put forward the theory that animals were "automata" (robots), without consciousness. He said that, unlike people, animals had no souls, no minds, no reason and were therefore unable to suffer or feel pain.

They know nothing

"[Animals] eat without pleasure, cry without pain, grow without knowing it; they desire nothing, fear nothing, know nothing."

Philosopher Nicolas Malebranche (1638–1715)

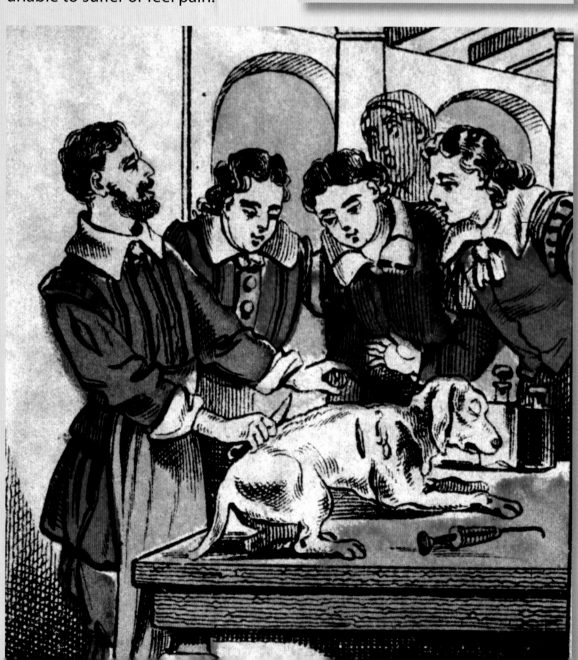

Feeling pleasure and pain

"There is no fundamental difference between man and the higher mammals in their mental faculties [abilities] ... The lower animals, like man, manifestly [clearly] feel pleasure and pain, happiness and misery."

Naturalist Charles Darwin, **The Descent of Man** *(1871)*

He also believed that the ability to reason distinguished humans from the animal kingdom. Descartes' theory confirmed what many people thought—that humans were beings with superior sensitivities—and it was used to justify the widespread practice of vivisection, as well as other types of casual cruelty toward animals.

Can they suffer?

At the end of the 18th century, a revolution overthrew the monarchy in France and prompted some observers to question what had

(Opposite) **In the early 17th century, the English physician William Harvey used vivisection (cutting into live animals) to explore the circulation of blood in mammals. Without effective anesthetics the animals must have suffered extreme pain.**

been up until then "the natural order of things." It challenged the notion that some people were born to be rich and others to be poor, some to rule and others to serve. This way of thinking would lead, eventually, to the abolition of slavery, a practice that many had regarded as natural and acceptable. The British philosopher Jeremy Bentham extended this reasoning to consider the way in which humans treated animals as "things." In response to the idea that animals lacked consciousness, he said: "…the question is not, Can they *reason*; nor, Can they *talk*, but Can they *suffer*?"

While Descartes' views still influence the attitudes of some people today, most of us accept that animals can suffer and do so on a daily basis (as do many humans). But does their ability to suffer mean they should have rights? Or is it simply our moral duty to treat them as well as we can? There is also the question about how we measure animal suffering. For example, how can we determine whether a relatively simple organism, such as a beetle or tiny fish, suffers to the same degree as a more complex animal, such as an elephant or orangutan?

Do they have rules?

One of the most common arguments against animal rights is that animals are incapable of behaving morally or of exercising moral judgement. As humans, we tend to associate rights with responsibility. If animals cannot behave responsibly, why should they have rights? In their natural state, carnivorous (meat-eating) animals hunt and kill one another without displaying compassion for their victims. People sometimes do this, too, as the many instances of genocide throughout history have shown. But human society has laws by which its members are held to account and punished for such acts of violence.

The argument goes that animals should not have rights because they cannot formulate codes of socially acceptable behavior. But are we, too, quick to assume that animals don't have social rules? Primatologists working with chimpanzees say they have witnessed evidence of so-called "human" qualities—for example empathy, emotion and attachment—in primate social groups.

Do they have an internal life?

Perhaps animals should not have rights because they can't talk and make demands, as humans can. But does the absence of speech mean that animals lack an internal life? Does it mean they don't think, plan and feel emotions—or does it simply suggest that they do these things differently from us? Should we only respect the rights of animals that behave like us? Certain animals, such as bats and dolphins, have sophisticated methods of communicating that we don't fully understand. Some animal rights supporters argue that many nonhuman mammals are similar to humans in terms of consciousness; in other words, they know they exist and they make conscious choices. Does it just suit us better to believe that they don't have internal worlds?

No sense of right and wrong

"Rights and responsibilities go together and I've yet to see a chimp imprisoned for stealing a banana because they [animals] don't have a moral sense of what's right and wrong."

Professor Steve Jones, University College London, 2007

(Opposite) **Primatologist Dr. Jane Goodall with a baby chimpanzee in Gombe Stream National Park, Tanzania. Her method of studying animals involves patient observation over long periods of time.**

Natural rights

"Some animals, certain primates especially, actually do think rather well ... Rights—especially natural rights—are things we have just by virtue of existing. They don't come with an invoice."

A. Barton Hinkle,
Richmond Times-Dispatch, *2011*

A Background to Animal Rights

In the ancient world, people used animals for food, clothing and as research subjects, as we do today. They also argued from both sides of the animal rights debate.

Natural hierarchy

"Plants are created for the sake of animals, and animals for the sake of men."

Aristotle

Universal spirit?

The Greek philosopher Aristotle (384–322 BCE) believed there was a "great chain of being," a natural hierarchy, with humans at the top, animals below and plants at the bottom. While Aristotle said animals lacked reason and humans owed them nothing, Pythagoras (c.569–475 BCE) said that humans and animals derived from the same elements—the universal spirit—and were therefore similar. A pupil of Aristotle, Theophrastus (c.371–287 BCE), said it was wrong to kill animals for food because they could reason, sense and feel just as humans do.

In ancient Greece attitudes to animals were shaped by religion, in which animal sacrifice played a major part. The ritual slaughter of animals was used to please the gods and anyone voicing opposition to it outraged the authorities. Pythagoras and Theophrastus both opposed animal sacrifice and urged respect for all living creatures.

Cruel entertainment

The citizens of ancient Rome had no such concerns. Animals were treated with extreme cruelty and

(Opposite) **The Coliseum in Rome, Italy, served as a public entertainment venue for nearly four centuries. "Sports" included battles to the death between wild animals.**

Opposition to sacrifice

"To what wicked habits does he accustom himself ... who cuts the throat of a calf, turning a deaf ear to its piteous moans. Or who has the heart to pierce the throat of a kid which utters cries like those of a child? Or kill the bird whom he has fed with his own hand? ... And is it not enough that such wickedness is committed by men? They have involved all the gods in this abomination [horror], and they believe that a Deity in the heavens can rejoice in the slaughter."

Ovid, on the use of animals in religious ritual

violence was glorified. For example, in 107 CE the Emperor Trajan staged a 123-day festival of "games," during which 11,000 animals, including lions, tigers, elephants and giraffes, were slaughtered. Meat-eating was a symbol of high status and animals were often cooked alive to "improve the flavor." There were a few critics. Ovid (43 BCE–17 CE), for example, saw cruelty to animals as a metaphor for mankind's violent behavior generally.

Practicing what you preach?

Religious thinking has influenced the treatment of animals down the centuries. The question of animal rights raises difficulties for religious people because it pits questions of moral conduct against traditional customs and practices.

Early Christianity taught that animals existed for human use.

This view was based on the Old Testament Book of Genesis, which states that God created man in his own image to rule over all Earth's creatures. It was believed that, unlike humans, animals had no soul. Today, the Christian view of the animal world tends to be a more sympathetic one. Most

The cow is a protected animal in India, where Hindus regard it as a symbol of life. Most rural families own a cow, which they rely on for milk, curds and ghee butter. But despite their special status, cows can often be seen wandering neglected around city streets.

Christians would see themselves working in partnership with nature rather than ruling over it.

Like Christianity, most other religions hold that animals are not equal to humans, but nevertheless should not be made to suffer. Although Hinduism does not put forward a particular view on the right way to treat animals, the majority of Hindus are vegetarian and Hindus do not eat beef. In India, cows are sacred, killing them is banned, and butchery and related work are restricted to people of low status.

Judaism and Islam both teach that animals should be treated with compassion, though they can be used for food. Jainism is the most animal-friendly faith. Jains are strict vegetarians who avoid intentional hurt to all living things.

Ritual slaughter

Many animal rights campaigners take particular issue with religious customs that govern methods of killing animals for food. Muslims are allowed to eat only animals that have been killed using the *halal* method. Judaism uses a similar practice, called *shechita*. Both methods involve cutting the throat of an animal with a single stroke and allowing it to bleed to death. While religious experts claim these practices are humane, many animal rights activists strongly disagree.

Reincarnation

Buddhism demonstrates the dilemma of religion versus animal rights:

- Buddhists believe in the doctrine of karma, which says that if people's souls are reincarnated (reborn) as animals, it is because of past wrongdoings

- animal souls must continue to be reborn as animals until they have exhausted the bad karma

- only when the souls are reborn as humans can the quest for a higher religious state be resumed

- an animal's inability to do anything to improve its bad karma has led some Buddhists to believe that animals are inferior to human beings, and are therefore entitled to fewer rights

15

Meat, Milk and Mass-Production

Is it acceptable to farm animals for food? For many people, eating meat is an important and pleasurable part of life. Other people believe eating meat is morally wrong. They argue that it is perfectly easy to lead a full, enjoyable life without it.

Healthy or unhealthy?

Those who argue in favor of animal farming say that humans are designed to eat meat; it is a useful source of protein, vitamins and minerals, some of which are difficult to obtain in a vegetarian diet. But opponents disagree. They say there is increasing evidence to suggest that certain types of animal products (processed meats, for example) are bad for us, and that a vegetarian diet provides a much healthier, guilt-free alternative to a meat-based one.

Killing for food

Supporters of animal farming point out that its history goes back to the dawn of time. Today, farming for meat provides a living to around 1.3 billion people worldwide and contributes about 40 percent to global agricultural output. However, some animal rights supporters argue that

The cost of meat

In 2006, the United Nations Food and Agriculture Organization reported the following:

- livestock generate more greenhouse gases than transport

- animal wastes, antibiotics and other medicines used to treat animals, fertilizers and the pesticides used to spray crops grown for animal feed are all major sources of pollution of both land and water

- livestock use 30 percent of Earth's entire land surface

- clearing forest for new pastures for grazing animals is a major cause of deforestation

raising animals in order to kill them for food is immoral and cruel. The animals have their lives cut short simply so that humans can enjoy eating them. They also say that eating meat is bad for the planet, since a diet containing meat requires up to three times more resources (land, water and fuel) than a vegetarian diet. What is more, the methane produced by

The meatpacking industry handles the slaughter of farm animals and the processing and packaging of meat for human consumption.

livestock contributes to global warming. If people stopped eating meat, animal cruelty could be avoided and large areas of grassland used as grazing for sheep and cattle could be turned over to tree-planting, crop production or wildlife.

Factory farming

Many animal rights activists argue that factory farming is the biggest cause of animal suffering in the world today. The animals are kept in vast sheds with no natural light. Pigs and veal calves are housed in crates and chickens in tiny cages in which they cannot turn round. Disease can spread fast in these

Behind the scenes

"If any kid ever realized what was involved in factory farming they would never touch meat again. I was so moved by the intelligence, sense of fun and personalities of the animals I worked with on *Babe* that by the end of the film I was a vegetarian."

James Cromwell, actor

The profit margin

"Farmers do not cage their hogs because of sadism [a desire to be cruel], but because dead pigs are a drag on the profit margin, and because being crushed by your mother really is an awful way to go. As is being eaten by your mother, which I've seen sows do to newborn pigs as well."

Blake Hurst, Missouri farmer, 2009

cramped conditions. To combat this, the animals are often dosed with antibiotics.

The laws regulating factory farming vary greatly from country to country. For example, in the European Union countries veal crates were banned in 2007. Calves up to eight weeks old are now kept in individual pens, where they can turn round and be in contact with other calves. After this, they are kept, often in sheds, in groups of up to 80 calves. Elsewhere in the world, however, conditions are less humane and in many countries, including the United States, the serious problems of factory farming persist. Apart from the animal suffering involved, activists argue that farming on this scale degrades the water, soil and air (see page 16).

(Opposite) **Intensively farmed pigs: in many countries pregnant sows are caged in rows of narrow stalls. Unable to express their natural behavior, they frequently perform pointless, repetitive motions such as biting the bars or trying to root at the concrete floor. Humane alternatives allow pigs the freedom to move around, either in large barns or outdoors.**

Managing nature

Worldwide, we are eating more meat today than ever before. One reason for this is that, as rapidly developing countries such as China and India become wealthier, their people eat more meat. Supporters of the factory system argue that intensive farming is necessary to produce enough cheap meat to feed the world. They also say that the critics don't understand animal behavior. Some farmers insist that, if left uncrated, mother sows may lie down and crush their own piglets to death. They say that nature is bloody, painful and messy, and it is the farmers' job to manage it as best they can. Opponents of factory farming argue that intensive systems should be replaced by humane alternatives that are kinder to the animals, safer for humans and better for the environment.

Good farming?

Some people argue that it is fine to eat meat if the animals lead a healthy, happy life and are killed humanely. They say it is important for humans to continue eating high-quality meat, free from chemical additives, because this means that good farming practices can be fostered. These include the keeping of free-range flocks and herds, where the young are reared in family groups and where animals can forage, graze, move freely and express their nature.

Supporters of free-range farming say that livestock play an important role in keeping wild areas clear and recycling plants, which is good for the environment and for wildlife. However, some animal rights activists say that many animals on free-range farms suffer the same procedures—debeaking, dehorning and castration without painkillers—as animals on factory farms.

Organic methods

Supporters of organic farming—the raising of animals and crops without the use of chemicals (drugs, fertilizers and pesticides,

Compassionate farming

"If meat-eating should ever become confined to those who do not care about animal suffering then compassionate farming would cease. All animals would be kept in battery conditions, and the righteous vegetarians would exert no economic pressure on farmers to change their ways. Where there are conscientious [principled] carnivores ... there is a motive to raise animals kindly ... Duty requires us, therefore, to eat our friends."

Roger Scruton, writer and philosopher, 2006

for example)—argue that it is much better for the environment because it does not interfere with the natural balance. However, some animal rights activists point out that, like factory farmers, organic farmers don't always allow animals enough space to thrive. Instead, they sometimes cram animals together in sheds or mud-filled lots to increase profits.

Animals as property

"Why do otherwise socially conscious consumers fail to ask if an animal's death is a fair price to pay to satisfy our carnivorous palates [appetites]? ... There's no denying that free-range systems are generally more concerned with animal welfare. But it's very difficult (if not impossible) for the owner of farm animals to give their "property" equal consideration because their status as property skews all consideration toward the owner's interest."

James McWilliams, associate professor of history at Texas State University, 2011

Transportation and slaughter

Finally, even free-range or organic animals have to be slaughtered. Animal rights supporters say that thousands of animals suffer cramped conditions and long periods of time without food and water during transportation to slaughterhouses. If not stunned properly, they also experience fear and pain at the point of death. Supporters of alternative farming methods say that they try to have the animals killed close to the farm. This avoids causing them excessive stress and reduces pollution and the expense of transportation.

Supporters of free-range farming say it enables animals to forage freely. Opponents argue that the animals' lives are still cut short by slaughter.

Animal products

What are the rights and wrongs of eating animal products such as milk, butter, cheese and eggs?

Dairy

Dairy products (milk, butter, cheese) have nutritional benefits and contain elements that are hard to find in a dairy-free diet. Perhaps the most important of these is calcium, which aids bone growth and health. However, some animal rights advocates believe that eating dairy foods is wrong.

Dairy cows are bred for high milk production. Critics argue that many cows are raised in confined spaces, which means they can't express their natural, social behavior. As cows only produce milk for around ten months after giving birth, they are impregnated every year, usually by artificial insemination. Dairy cows are productive for around three years, after which they are killed for meat. Female calves are kept to restock the herd, but male calves are either killed or sold on to the veal industry (see page 19).

Eggs

Worldwide, over 60 percent of the eggs for sale in shops are laid by caged hens. Throughout the EU, the battery hen system is being replaced by laying cages (see panel). Defenders of both systems say they are more hygienic in food safety terms than free-range conditions. This is because egg production is closely monitored and the eggs are quickly removed from laying hens. The cage system also protects hens from predators and diseases that can be spread by wild birds.

Egg facts

- **battery hens:** kept in tiny cages cannot forage for food, nest, roost or dust-bathe

- **laying cage system:** gives the hens slightly larger cages, together with nest boxes and perches

- **barn-laid eggs:** produced by hens kept in large (often overcrowded) sheds where they have perches and litter to scratch in

- **free-range eggs:** laid by hens that have daytime access to outdoor runs, with nest boxes, perches and litter

- **organic eggs:** laid by free-range hens that are given only organic feed, and with restrictions on the use of antibiotics

However, critics of the battery system say that the new laying cages are only slightly better than the old ones. In the UK, a typical cage holds four or five hens in a space the size of an A4 sheet of

Battery hen cages are usually so small that the hens cannot turn round or stretch their wings.

paper for each bird. The cage is just high enough for the hens to stand upright. In the U.S., the space allowed for each bird is even smaller.

Animals and Science

Should animals be used in scientific experiments? Some people say no, not under any circumstances. Some say yes, in certain instances; others say it is necessary to test on animals because doing so saves many human lives. What about the use of animals in safety tests for products such as cosmetics or household cleaners? Is this acceptable as long as humane laws are observed? Or should we use alternative methods of testing that don't involve animals?

Safety tests

There are three main reasons why animals are used in scientific experimentation. The first is for general research into the biology of an animal, and the action of certain diseases within its body; the

second is to test the safety of new drugs and vaccines before they are tried out on human subjects. The third is to test the safety of a range of products, for example food additives, household chemicals or fertilizers, for their potential harm to animals, humans and the environment.

Scientists argue that experiments on animals occur only at the end of a long process of other safety tests. These may include testing the product "in vitro" (in a test tube), or using a computer program to simulate what might happen to the drug or product inside the body. They say that everything is done to minimize the risk of pain and distress to the animals involved. Health and safety concerns, together with the fear of legal action should things go wrong in human trials, means that more animals are likely to be used in the future (see page 43).

Critics argue that animal testing is cruel and unnecessary. They question the accuracy of results produced by doing tests on animals that are then applied to

Cosmetic catastrophe

In 1933, over a dozen women in the U.S. became blind after using a mascara called Lash Lure, which contained an untested chemical. At the time, there were no regulations to ensure the safety of products. The chemical caused horrific blisters, abscesses and ulcers on the women's faces, eyelids and eyes. In one case, the ulcers were so severe that the woman developed a bacterial infection and died. Today, the law requires cosmetics manufacturers to prove the safety of their products. For the majority, this involves testing on animals, though the number of animals used for cosmetic testing has been greatly reduced in recent years.

humans. For example, they say that some drugs may be effective, or dangerous, in animals but not in humans, and the other way around. They say it is no more ethical to give an animal a life-threatening illness during vaccine testing than it is to give it to a human.

(Opposite) **In the UK, rodents make up around 84 percent of the animals used in scientific experiments. Mice are the most popular subjects as they are easy to handle, small and can reproduce rapidly.**

Genetic engineering

Some tests on animals are designed to give us a better understanding of biology and physiology; others may have a direct impact on life in the future. These tests involve genetic engineering—changing the genetic code, or DNA, of a selected animal for a specific purpose. Examples of genetic engineering include xenografting (introducing the DNA of one species into another), cloning (using the DNA of an animal to produce an identical animal) and manipulation (the changing of animal DNA). This work helps scientists to understand more about how genes function.

Genetically modified animals

Animals that are deliberately bred for research by having their genes altered in some way are known as genetically modified animals. They are usually mice or rats. Some have genes deleted or turned off (these are called "knockout" animals); others have genes added (these are called "transgenic" animals). These animals can provide vital information about diseases in humans that are caused by faulty

New possibilities

"Already we have taken the spider's web gene and put it into a goat, which means that we can create spider's web sticky gunk in the milk of the goat and we can turn that into a new suture [stitching] material for surgeons..."

Patrick Dixon, author and business consultant, 2007

genes, such as cystic fibrosis or sickle cell disease. Other animals are genetically modified to develop diseases, such as cancer.

Arguments for and against

Supporters of genetic engineering in animals point to its many benefits for humans. They say it helps scientists to work out how to eliminate serious illnesses in both humans and animals. It may also be used to combat the spread of disease. Critics say that, apart from the cruelty of these tests, genetic engineering involves an unnatural "mixing" between species that many people find morally wrong and even repulsive. Does genetic engineering reduce

Mad, wretched practice

"The mad, wretched practice of inserting genes into the embryos of another to create 'transgenic animals' has already produced moribundly [seriously] ill entities with new shapes and forms beset with terribly hideous diseases... "

Dr. Moneim Fadali,
U.S. heart surgeon

animals to mere objects and is it wrong to "tamper with nature" in this way? Some people believe that it is unethical to modify an animal's genetic makeup for a specific purpose, without knowing in advance if there will be any side effects that will cause it to suffer.

Dr. Ian Wilmut, a leading scientist at the Roslin Institute in Edinburgh, Scotland, poses with Dolly, a cloned sheep. In 1996, Dolly became the first animal to be cloned from DNA taken from an adult animal.

Wild Animals

Human behavior affects the lives of animals in the wild. On the one hand, the ever-increasing human population destroys animal habitats in its quest for natural resources. On the other hand, many animal species would now be extinct if it had not been for human help. So do we have responsibilities toward wild animals?

Zoos

Long ago, rulers kept large collections of wild animals simply to demonstrate their power. In the 1800s there was a surge in the popularity of public zoos, where people could come and look at animals for entertainment. Today, the thinking behind zoos has shifted, but even so standards vary enormously. At best they are well-financed, well-run ventures where animals have relative freedom and plenty of stimulation; at worst they are private concerns run on a shoestring by animal collectors who keep their captives in appalling conditions.

Vital work

"As wild populations of elephants continue to decline in Africa and Asia, AZA accredited zoos are playing a vital role as stewards of an important part of the world's heritage. While supporting conservation programs in the wild, AZA institutions are also holding 290 African and Asian elephants in 73 institutions and are dedicated to caring for these animals in a humane and science-based manner."

American Association of Zoos and Aquariums (AZA) Web site, 2011

Supporters of zoos say they fulfill a vital role, keeping alive many species threatened with extinction in the wild. Many zoos work to rehabilitate animals where possible and carry out important research into conservation. They argue that they offer visitors both entertainment and education, and help to develop more compassionate attitudes toward animals.

Right to freedom

Opponents of zoos say that keeping any animal in an enclosure severely restricts its right to freedom. They believe that rehabilitating animals into the wild often fails because animals in zoos become used to captivity and find it hard to readjust. This makes them vulnerable to predators. Opponents also argue there is no evidence to suggest that people who visit zoos are any better informed about animal rights than people who don't visit them.

A brown bear at Warsaw Zoo in Poland: zoos want interesting sights to attract the crowds, but many people believe that keeping large animals captive is cruel.

Dumping grounds

"An article in *US News* (August 5, 2002) exposed the widespread dumping of 'surplus' animals by some of America's leading zoos. The reporter even found two endangered gibbons in a filthy cage with no water, in a bankrupt roadside zoo just off Interstate 35 in Texas."

Dale Jamieson,
Against Zoos, *2006*

Culling

Culling is the deliberate reduction of wild animal numbers by humans. The arguments in favor of culling include the preservation of other species. In 2003, for example, a cull of hedgehogs in the Western Isles of Scotland was carried out to protect wading birds on the islands—it was thought that the hedgehogs were eating the birds' eggs. Other reasons for culling include the protection of people's livelihoods and food sources, for example, farmers whose crops are being eaten by deer and rabbits. Many people also believe that culling stops the spread of disease and keeps the animals that are left fit and strong.

Badgers and bears

Culling provokes fierce debate in many countries around the world. In the UK, it is widely believed that badgers carry a form of tuberculosis

A female harp seal with her pup: each year in Canada, hundreds of thousands of young harp seals are killed for their skins. The government claims that the seals need to be culled to protect the North Atlantic cod fisheries. Opponents of the cull argue that the decline in fish stocks is the result of overfishing by humans, not seals.

A way of life?

People in Canada have been hunting seals for at least 4,000 years. Seal meat is still an important part of the diet of the Inuit people. The Inuit also use seal pelts (skins) for clothing and seal oil for cooking and as a fuel. Traditional Inuit hunting of adult ring seals (as opposed to young harp seals) accounts for 3 percent of the total Canadian seal hunt. Inuit representatives argue that a ban on seal hunting in the 1980s wrecked their economy; they say that they will continue to hunt because it is a vital part of their way of life.

(TB) that they pass on to cattle. Many farmers want the right to kill badgers in order to control the spread of TB. But new research has shown that badger culls may actually increase the numbers of cases of TB in cattle because culling allows surviving, infected badgers to roam outside their usual territories.

In the U.S., numbers of black bears have increased in recent years, and many states permit annual hunts. The main reason given for these hunts is the need to keep the bear population under control so that bears do not become a nuisance to people in residential areas. Opponents of the hunts accuse state officials of overestimating the numbers of bears, and the number of nuisance attacks on people. They are particularly critical of hunts in springtime, which can leave young bear cubs orphaned and unable to survive.

No simple solutions?

Opponents of culling include many people who object to the mass killing of animals if they are not being eaten or otherwise used. They say that culls interfere with the balance of nature and that animals are quite capable of limiting their own numbers. They believe that some of the methods used, such as clubbing seals to death, are brutal. They argue that there are in many cases humane alternatives to culling, for example noisemaking machines that deter seals from damaging fishing nets. In any case, there is very rarely a single solution to any problem, as shown by the Scottish hedgehog cull. This was ultimately ineffective because other animals apart from the hedgehogs were also found to be eating the birds' eggs.

The Pleasure Principle

Many people accept the need to raise animals for food, or to use them in medical research. But what about the use of animals and animal products simply for enjoyment? Some people believe it is acceptable to wear animal fur, or to train animals for entertainment and sports. Millions of people around the world keep animals as pets. Their opponents say that most of these practices are exploitative and wrong.

Fur

Fur coats and trimmings fluctuate in popularity depending on the whim of the fashion industry. Fans of fur say it looks beautiful and is incredibly warm. Those in favor of fur say that most of the animals used (approximately 85 percent) are farmed. They say that in order to produce beautiful fur, the animals must be happy and healthy, so it makes good business sense to ensure welfare standards are high.

The fur industry has long been a prime target for animal rights activists. Organizations such as People for the Ethical Treatment of Animals (PETA) oppose any use of animal fur or skins to make clothes, shoes or handbags. PETA points out that many animals on fur farms and in the wild are killed inhumanely, by electrocution, trapping, drowning or beating. Some are skinned alive and left to die.

Turning tide?

Nevertheless, an opinion poll in the United States found that the percentage of people in favor of

Real price of fur?

"The real price of fur must be measured in deaths—not dollars. To make one fur coat you must kill at least 55 wild mink, 35 ranched mink, 40 sables, 11 lynx, 18 red foxes, 11 silver foxes, 100 chinchillas, 30 rex rabbits, 9 beavers, 30 muskrats, 15 bobcats, 25 skunks, 14 otters, 125 ermines, 30 possums, 100 squirrels, or 27 raccoons."

From the Defense of Animals Web site, 2011

A PETA activist disrupts a catwalk show in a demonstration against the use of fur by fashion designers. The animal rights group PETA often employs such eye-catching strategies to get its message across.

using animal fur increased from 54 percent in 2008 to 61 percent in 2009. To explain this shift, fur industry insiders point to the "harassing tactics" that have been used by some animal rights militants. Such tactics, including arson (starting fires), bombings and vandalism, certainly keep the issue in the news. But extreme acts of violence may also turn public opinion against the anti-fur campaign.

While many people oppose wearing fur, a great number of us routinely wear leather. Every year, the hides of billions of slaughtered animals are used in the leather industry. Is the fact that the animals are also used for meat enough to justify the wearing of leather?

Highest standards of care?

"Animal welfare is a top priority for the people working in the fur industry because when animals provide us with a wide range of products and services, we have a responsibility to ensure the highest standards of care and prevent unnecessary suffering."

From the Fur Council of Canada Web site, 2011

Four-legged friends

Should we keep animals as pets? On one side of this argument we know that pets are beneficial for humans: they enrich our lives by offering companionship and their presence in the home reduces stress. Pets such as dogs help keep us healthy (if we take them for regular walks, that is!). The other side of the argument is that the keeping of pets is selfish because many pet owners treat animals as property to do with as they please.

The benefits

Establishing a bond with an animal can vastly improve a person's mental well-being—from children with behavioral difficulties to older people with Alzheimer's or depression. Pets encourage playfulness, satisfy the need to touch and be touched, and give nonjudgmental warmth and affection. Do the many benefits of pet ownership outweigh the sometimes negative effects on the pets themselves?

Cruelty and neglect

Opponents of pet ownership say that while many loving owners treat their pets with care and respect, there is widespread cruelty and neglect. The number of unwanted animals in rescue shelters proves how casually some people abandon their pets. In particular, animal rights activists highlight the desire for pedigree animals as particularly damaging. Such intensive breeding can cause serious health problems. The high demand for particular breeds of dog may encourage the growth of businesses such as puppy mills—

Compassionate farming

"The human–animal bond bypasses the intellect and goes straight to the heart and emotions and nurtures us in ways that nothing else can ... We've seen this from coast to coast, whether it's disabled children at a riding center in California or a nursing home in Minnesota, where a woman with Alzheimer's could not recognize her husband but she could recognize their beloved dog."

Karin Winegar Saved: **Rescued Animals and the Lives They Transform,** *2008*

farms where female dogs are condemned to produce litter after litter, often in terrible conditions. These puppy farms exist primarily to make big profits, mass-producing puppies for sale mainly via dealers or over the Internet.

Rescue shelters look after homeless animals, including dogs, cats, horses and rabbits. They rely on donations and on people coming forward to give pets loving homes.

Selfish desire?

"This selfish desire to possess animals and receive love from them causes immeasurable suffering, which results from manipulating their breeding, selling or giving them away casually, and depriving them of the opportunity to engage in their natural behavior."

From the PETA Web site, 2011

Animals in entertainment

From the chariot races of Roman times to the horse races of today, the history of animals in entertainment is a long and colorful one. Is it acceptable to use animals in entertainment, circuses and sports, or is it exploitative and cruel?

People who support the use of animals in entertainment say that trainers develop close relationships with their animals and treat them well. They say the animals enjoy the stimulation of performing or the exercise of racing. They argue that these highly trained animals are well-fed and pampered, whereas it is possible that in the wild they would be struggling for survival.

Blood sports

In 1839, the London Police Act banned cockfighting and the baiting of lions, bears, badgers, dogs and other animals in the UK. At the time, many people would have argued that these blood sports were acceptable forms of entertainment. Although illegal in most countries, some of these cruel activities are still practiced today.

Having fun?

There are many arguments against the use of animals in entertainment. Some animal rights campaigners argue that circus animals live in chains when they are not performing. They point out that whips and bullhooks (long-handled, sharp hooks) are used to inflict pain during training. Similarly, electrical prods and sharp spurs are used on horses and cows in rodeos. Calf-roping events in rodeos have resulted in punctured lungs, internal bleeding, paralysis and broken necks. The sport of bullfighting may be a traditional art and a test of human skill and courage, but it relies on an unequal fight between an armed matador (bullfighter) and a bull that almost always ends with the death of the bull.

Opponents of dog and horse racing argue that these sports have little to do with animal welfare and everything to do with money. They say that racing greyhounds are kept in cages for more than 20 hours a day. Sometimes dogs who are considered too slow to race are sold to research facilities or killed. More racehorses are bred than can prove profitable on the racetrack. As a result, hundreds of racehorses are slaughtered every year.

(Opposite) **A young woman ropes a calf in a rodeo competition. Rodeo organizations monitor events closely and insist that few calves are injured in the sport.**

Hunting

Is it acceptable to hunt animals for sport? In 2005 hunting with dogs was banned in the UK, but evidence suggests that people are continuing to hunt, which proves that the ban is very difficult to enforce. Those in favor of hunting say it is a traditional pastime that provides employment

Why hunt?

"I ask people why they have deer heads on their walls. They always say because it's such a beautiful animal. There you go. I think my mother is attractive, but I have photographs of her."

Comedienne Ellen DeGeneres

for a large number of people who enjoy the ritual and thrill of the chase. They say it is a natural act—after all, wild animals hunt and kill one another, so it is nonsensical to argue that humans should not hunt. They say it is an effective way of controlling animals such as foxes, rabbits, mink and deer, all of which cause damage to farmers' livelihoods, either by killing farm animals or eating crops. Hunters say it is the most humane method of pest control, as the animals are killed quickly, not left injured.

Pain and fear

Opponents say that hunting is wrong because the animals suffer pain and fear during the chase and (especially in the case of larger mammals, such as deer) at the kill. They say it is morally wrong to hunt for fun and that there are other, more effective ways of controlling pests. They say the animal rights argument outweighs the case in favor of tradition and pleasure. Throughout history, a number of traditional practices that people used to enjoy—for example, public executions and the

(Opposite) **Supporters of deer hunting say that it is an effective form of management. They argue that natural deer predators no longer exist in many areas, so hunters are needed to keep the deer population in check.**

I am a hunter

"I hunt because I am a hunter. Clearly such natural participation in God's miraculous creation is the last perfect, pure and positive environmental activity available to mankind. Balancing the annual wildlife explosion through respectful sustainable yield utility [hunting] is universally known to be the perfection that it is. Know it, cherish it, celebrate it and by all means, do it. Life is not meant to be a spectator sport, y'all."

Rock guitarist Ted Nugent, 2010

enslavement of other humans—were banned because people finally accepted they were wrong. Thousands of years ago, humans hunted animals in order to survive. Opponents of hunting say that in the vast majority of cases this argument does not apply today, yet recreational hunting continues to be permitted in many national parks, endangering wildlife.

Rights and Wrongs

In 1975, a book called *Animal Liberation* by the philosopher Peter Singer addressed the question of "the tyranny of humans over nonhuman animals." Singer said the refusal to count animal suffering as equal to human suffering was "speciesism." He argued that just as racism is a prejudice in favor of your own race, speciesism is a prejudice in favor of your own species, and therefore morally wrong. Singer's reasoning led to the growth of a more militant animal rights movement.

Direct action

While most animal rights activists are peaceful, some believe that the only way to get their message across is through direct action and shock tactics. A small number of violent incidents have shown that a minority are willing to harm themselves and others to further their cause. Militants have staged break-ins of research facilities (in order to free the animals there), threatened scientists involved in animal testing and carried out fire- and letter-bombings.

Opponents say that violence and threats are unacceptable as well as against the law. But activists argue that there is still no international agreement on laws governing animal experimentation. While laws

Respectful treatment

"Some critics have said that the animal rights movement is corroded [weakened] by the attitudes of people who do not like other human beings. It's time to consider this criticism seriously. Fundamentally there is no difference between the idea of treating other human beings respectfully and treating other animals respectfully."

Professor Gary Francione, specialist in animal rights and law

Animal rights activists chant and wave placards in a protest against bullfighting in Barcelona, Spain, in 2010. This protest was successful—bullfighting is now banned in the Catalan region of Spain.

are strict in the UK, they are less so in the U.S. and some South American countries have none. Activists say that milder forms of protest, such as letter-writing, petitions and marches, don't make the headlines. Groups such as PETA deliberately use campaigns designed to shock— posters of glamorous models holding skinned and bloody

Effective tactics

"Our non-violent tactics are not as effective. We ask nicely for years and get nothing. Someone makes a threat, and it works."

PETA president Ingrid Newkirk, US News & World Report, *April 2002*

animals, for example—in order to grab media attention.

The way forward

Is it vital to the future of humanity that we continue to use animals in the way we do? Or should we change our behavior toward other species? Is it nonsensical to argue that animals should have rights?

Moral progress

"The greatness of a nation and its moral progress can be judged by the way its animals are treated."

Mahatma Gandhi, leader of the nationalist movement against British rule in India

Or has our understanding of animal psychology improved to such an extent that we need to reconsider how we treat other living beings?

An end to suffering?

Some scientists believe that genetic engineering may solve all the ethical problems of laboratory experiments on animals. They aim to create a genetically engineered mammal that lacks sentience (feeling), but is otherwise identical to normal experimental animals. They say that such an animal could not suffer whatever was done to it, so the moral problem of performing experiments on animals would be avoided. Certainly, as new drugs continue to be trialled, it is likely that animal testing will continue for some time to come.

A compassionate future

Others argue that for the sake of the planet, humans need to tame their competitive urges and be more compassionate. Researchers say that social animals—elephants, dolphins, baboons, chimpanzees and hyenas—take part in dynamic societies made up of individuals.

(Opposite) A pod of dolphins leaping out of the water in the Indian Ocean. Dolphins communicate with each other by way of clicks and whistles, and they frequently display cooperative behavior.

Last resort

"No one wants to use animals in research, and no one would use them unnecessarily. Animal research is considered a last resort, to be used only when there is no alternative method."

www.understanding animalresearch.org. uk/about_research

Their lives appear to be full of feelings, decisions and intentions. Although these animal groups are competitive, they are also cooperative because the animals instinctively work together to survive. Researchers say we could learn a lot from them.

Is it unrealistic to expect animals to be granted rights? Most people believe it is, and it is certainly difficult to imagine how the world would be organized if all animals had equal rights with humans. Others, however, believe that the measure of a healthy society is determined by the way it cares for its vulnerable members, such as children, older people and animals.

Glossary

additive a substance that is added to something in order to improve, strengthen or change it

Alzheimer's a brain disease, usually affecting older people, that results in memory loss, confusion and changes in personality

animal rights a belief system that opposes the exploitation of animals

antibiotics drugs for treating infections caused by tiny organisms called bacteria

artificial insemination the process of placing sperm from a male into the reproductive organs of a female

castration the removal of the testes (reproductive organs) of a male animal

compassionate sympathetic to the feelings of others

conservation in relation to wildlife, a movement to protect and preserve all types of animals and plants, and their habitats

culling selecting animals to kill

cystic fibrosis a disease that appears usually in early childhood and is marked by faulty digestion and difficulty in breathing

debeaking the removal of the tip of the beak to prevent fighting among battery hens

dehorning the removal of a cow's horns to prevent damage to other livestock among intensively farmed animals

DNA (de-oxyribonucleic acid) the chemical that carries genetic information inside the nucleus of a cell

embryo an animal in the early stages of growth before birth or hatching

empathy being aware of and sharing another's feelings and emotions

extinction the end of an organism, or a group of organisms, usually marked by the death of the last individual of the species

gene a length of DNA that gives a specific characteristic to an individual

genocide the deliberate destruction of a particular group of people

global warming the increase over time of the average temperature of Earth's atmosphere and oceans

hierarchy the arrangement of people or things into ranks or classes

humane marked by compassion, sympathy or consideration for humans or animals

karma a belief in Hinduism and Buddhism that your actions, good or bad, determine what happens to you in future lives

militant aggressively active

moral able to choose between right and wrong

philosopher a person who studies the nature of knowledge, reality and existence

physiology the way in which a living organism or part of the body functions

primates mammals with hands and feet that grasp, relatively large brains and three-dimensional vision

primatologists scientists who study the behavior of apes and monkeys

psychology the ways in which an individual or group thinks and behaves

rehabilitate to restore to good health and normal life

species a group of organisms that share similar characteristics and can breed with each other

vaccine a preparation of a disease that is used as a medical treatment to give immunity to that disease

veal a young calf or its flesh for use as meat

vivisection the use of live animals in medical experiments

For More Information

Books

Your Environment: Animal Rights Julia Allen and Margaret Iggulden,
    Franklin Watts 2008

Global Questions: Do Animals Have Rights? Yolanda Brooks, Franklin
    Watts 2008

Do Animals Have Rights? Alison Hills, Icon Books 2005

World Issues: Animal Rights Penny Tripp, Chrysalis 2005

Web Sites

Due to the changing nature of Internet links, Rosen Publishing has
developed an online list of Web sites related to the subject of this
book. This site is updated regularly. Please use this link to access
the list:

http://www.rosenlinks.com/BSOS/Anim

Index

Bold entries indicate pictures